howto marketing

series of business self-help books written by practitioners

the little cook book of social media marketing

by Thom Poole

written by Thomas F Poole © 2011 Thom Poole

first published by Lulu in 2011

ISBN: 978-1-4477-0892-6

for Emma
for your support in my efforts to
build more sociable marketing

contents

what is *social media*?

" *social media* is just a buzzword until you come up with a plan. "

Zach Dunn

be sociable

the best way to explain *social media* is to look at its constituent parts.   media is the channel for communication – you will be familiar will newspapers, radio or television.

on the web, media would be your website, but if you can interact with your customers, or if they can interact with one another, you are entering the world of *social media*.

social media incorporates the online technology and methods with which people can share content, personal opinions, swap different ideas of world issues and generally discuss the evolution of media in itself.

social media website content can come in many shapes and forms:

- text - text is often used to put across opinions or write blog posts
- images - images and photos can display anything from holiday photos to shots by professional photographers
- audio - social media lets you create podcasts for users to download
- video - video sites mean that you'll be able to record a video of your child's birthday for friends all over the world to see

a few examples of the most popular types of *social media* websites are:

social networking - websites that allows you to create a personal profile then chat, discuss and share information with others such as friends and family. popular examples of social networking sites are MySpace, Bebo and Facebook.

wikis - wikis are websites that allow you to create, edit and share information about a subject or topic. wikipedia is one of the world's most popular wikis.

video sharing - video-sharing sites allow you to upload and share your personal videos with the rest of the web community. a popular example of a video sharing website is YouTube.

photo sharing - photo sharing websites allow users to upload pictures and images to a personal account which can then be viewed by web users the world over. Flickr acts as a great example of a successful photo-sharing site.

news aggregation - news aggregators provide a list of the latest news stories published by users from a range of different websites. Digg is one of the web's largest news aggregators with one of the most dedicated communities.

social bookmarking - social bookmarking sites allow users to publicly bookmark web pages they find valuable in order to share them with other internet users.

online gaming - online gaming is often based around communities. World of Warcraft is prime example of online gaming.

presence apps - these websites allow you to post micro blog-like posts to announce what you are currently doing. Twitter is a good example of a presence app.

source: bigmouthmedia.com

social media marketing

social media marketing is the process of marketing through social media sites like Twitter, Facebook and YouTube. *social media marketing* is able to connect and interact on a much more personalised and dynamic level than through traditional marketing by using the social aspect of the web.

a *social media marketing* strategy can be as simple as having a company blog, a Twitter account, or incorporating "Digg This" and "Tweet This" tags to the end of articles.

it can also be as complicated as having a full *social media* campaign that encompasses blogs, microblogs (Twitter), social networking and viral videos (YouTube).

the little cook book of social media marketing

why is *social media marketing* important?

"social networks aren't about websites.   they're about experiences.
Mike DiLorenzo
NHL social media marketing director

some numbers

there are more than   **110 million blogs**   being tracked by Technorati.

source: http://www.technorati.com

there are an estimated   **2 billion videos**   being watched each day on the video sharing website, YouTube.

source: http://mashable.com/2010/05/17/youtube-2-billion-views

there are over   **500 million users**   on Facebook, that means it is now used by 1 in every 13 people on earth, with over 250 million of them (over 50%) who log in every day.   the average user still has about 130 friends.

source: http://www.digitalbuzzblog.com/facebook-statistics-stats-facts-2011/

there are   **175 million**   registered users on Twitter.   **119 million**   Twitter accounts follow one or more other accounts.   **85 million** accounts have one or more followers.

source: http://technolog.msnbc.msn.com/_news/2011/04/01

socially vital

an online marketing campaign is made of many vital elements, one of them being having a good content marketing strategy in place. delivering the right message to the target audience plays a crucial role in the overall execution of your digital marketing programme.

it's a common thought that there's a certain connection between the size of a network and the effectiveness of that marketing campaign. however, when we talk about *social media*, quality plays a bigger role than quantity.

this is why you need to gather insight and learn more about your audience when creating a *social media* content strategy. this can be achieved through effective participation, employing various monitoring tools, analysing and studying the traffic generated through social media sites and using third party data reporting tools.

source: http://promotedprofits.com/why-social-media-marketing-is-so-important

customer engagement

not everyone who arrives at a retail site is ready to make a purchase.

most retailers want to turn a one-time buyer into a lifelong customer, and *social media* can play a very significant role in helping a shopper become emotionally attached to a retail brand and, ultimately, make a retailer's destination part of the customer's online routine.

content has a role to play here, too.   retailers can promote their own staff and expert customers with informative blogs that establish the company's commitment and authority.

but conversation and interaction are equally important. forums can become a valuable source of insight for shoppers, product owners and retailers alike.

social networking and group features can encourage like-minded people to build personal relationships around topics that are central to the retailer's business.

the little cook book of social media marketing

ingredients of *social media marketing?*

"*social networking* that matters is helping people archive their goals. doing it reliably and repeatability so that over time people have an interest in helping you achieve your goals."

Seth Godin, Seth's Blog

social characteristics

participation

social networks encourage contributions and feedback from anyone who is interested. it blurs the line between the media and audience.

openness

most *social networking* services are open to feedback and participation.   they encourage voting, comments and the sharing of information.   there are rarely any barriers to accessing and making use of content – password-protected content is frowned on.

conversation

whilst traditional media is about "broadcasting" (content transmitted or distributed to an audience) *social media* is better seen as a two-way conversation.

community

social media allows communities to form quickly and communicate effectively.   communities share common interests.

connectedness

most kinds of *social media* thrive on their connectedness, making use of links to other.

source: What is Social media? by Antony Mayfield

success guide

social media is any online network where people can join and communicate with each other. *social media marketing* is the act of leveraging the *social media* platforms to promote a product or a service in order to increase your visibility and credibility and ultimately increase your sales.

these are seven of the most vital ingredients for a successful *social media marketing* campaign:

1. **blog**

   your blog is the centre of all your online activity so it's vital to have one that integrates well with all the other *social networks*.

2. **opt-in**

   a highly noticeable opt-in box will help build your list and therefore reach. to encourage people to opt-in you may need to give them some form of freebie to sign-up.

3. **autoresponder programme**

   use this to send regular bulletins to your audiences. also use it to thank people for signing up for the information.

4. **multiple *social network* accounts**

   sign-up to all the relevant social networks, and visit them regularly. follow others generously and learn from them.

the little cook book of social media marketing

5. **link your blog back to your *social network* pages**

   social media is all about creating links, and the links you create between your various accounts, you can help interested audiences find relevant information.

6. **join *social bookmarking* sites**

   whenever you find interesting articles, make it visible to your audiences. use services such as Tasty, Digg, Dilgo and Technorati.

7. **submit articles to an ezine site regularly**

   with approximately 15 million unique users, your articles will build your reputation, and your following.

   source: http://boostingwebtraffic.com

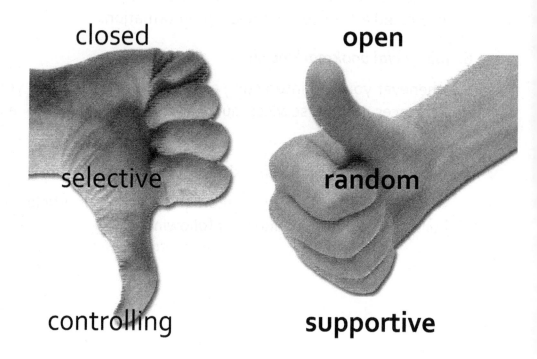

closed   **open**

selective   random

controlling   **supportive**

traditionally businesses are closed, selective, and controlling but to survive and prosper in the *social media* era they must become **open**, **random** and **supportive**.

"when you jump into a network, you have to change all of those things," says Thomas Power co-founder of ecademy and 'inventor' of ORS. "you have to be open. you have to accept everything that comes at you. you have to be random. the disorder that things arrive in your life. completely chaotic. and you have to be supportive of everyone around you."

six degrees of separation

the unproven theory that states that anyone on the planet can be connected to any other person on the planet through a chain of acquaintances.   the theory was first proposed by the Hungarian writer – Frigyes Karinthy in 1929.

this is the core of the business networking site – LinkedIn, where members are encouraged to link to others for recommendations and referrals in extended networks.

my own LinkedIn network of over 500 contacts has 186,800 contacts just two degrees away (friends of friends).   a third degree pushes my network to almost 8 million – and that is only half way!

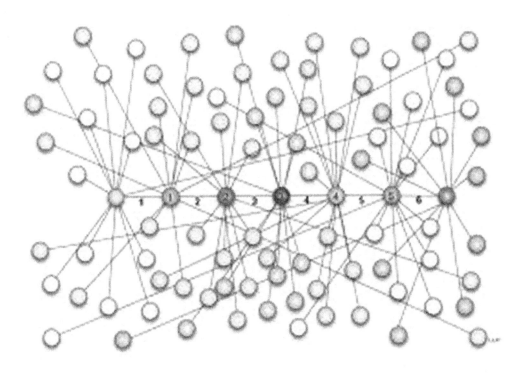

the little cook book of social media marketing

social media marketing recipes

"networking is not about hunting. it is about farming. it's about cultivating relationships. don't engage in 'premature solicitation'. you'll be a better networker if you remember that."

Dr. Ivan Misner
bestselling author & founder of BNI

the 'social family'

social media incorporates the online technology and methods through which people can share content, personal opinions, swap different perspectives and insights into issues that people feel passionate about.

social media website content can come in many shapes and forms:

- **text** - often used to put across opinions or write blog posts.
- **images and photos** - displaying anything from holiday photos to shots by professional photographers.
- **audio** - *social media* lets you create podcasts for users to download.
- **video** – sites that allow you to share your video programme or production.
- **slideshows** – sharing presentations that have been created for particular audiences.

blogging

a blog is a hierarchy of text, images, media objects and data, arranged chronologically so that it can be viewed in a html browser. it is a form of online diary/journal.

blogs can serve as an extension of traditional media.   just as a marketer would send review copies to traditional media outlets like newspapers and magazines, they can now also be sent to popular blogs on a particular subject.

tips for blog writing

1. make your opinion known

    people like blogs, they like blogs because they are written by people and not faceless organisations.   people want to know what people think, crazy as it sounds they want to know what you think.   tell them exactly what you think using the least amount of words possible.

2. link like crazy

    support your post with links to other web pages that are contextual to your post.

3. write less

    give the maximum amount of information with the least amount of words.   time is finite and people are infinitely busy. blast your knowledge into the reader at the speed of sound.

the little cook book of social media marketing

4. 250 is enough

a long post is easier to forget and harder to get into. a short post is the opposite so try to limit your posts to 250 words.

5. make headlines snappy

contain your whole argument in your headline. check out national newspapers to see how they do it.

6. include bullet point lists

we all love lists, it structures the information in an easily digestible format.

7. make your posts easy to scan

every few paragraphs insert a sub heading. make sentences and headlines short and to the point.

8. be consistent with your style

    people like to know what to expect, once you have settled on a style for your audience stick to it.

9. litter the post with keywords.

    think about what keywords people would use to search for your post and include them in the body text and headers. make sure the keyword placement is natural and does not seem out of place.

10. edit your post

    good writing is in the editing.   before you hit the submit button, re-read your post and cut out the stuff that you don't need.

    source: Darren Rowse - http://www.problogger.net

the little cook book of social media marketing

microblogging

Twitter is the most famous microblogging service. Twitter is a tool through which subscribers can further reach their audiences, real-time. users can hear and express thought leadership, broadcast their messages, connect to the influencers both on their desktop and through their mobile units, among other things.

the real business uses of the twitter can be identified as follows:

- extending the reach for those individuals or companies that already have a blogging strategy in place, and want to deepen or further ties.

- retailers announcing sales and deals.

- increasing the ability for frequent updates to blogs or web sites or news.

- building consensus or a community of supporters.

- building a buzz. get people talking about what you are doing.

- updating breaking news. be seen to be proactive at conferences or events.

- updating your network to shape your own personal branding.

source: Ann Handley on MarketingProfs

the little cook book of social media marketing

Twitter statistics

- **55% female** tweeters (source: Quantcast)

- **75 million users** (Jan 2010, source: Comscore)

- approx. **50 million tweets** per day (source: Twitter)

- over **20% of users are active** (source: the metric system)

- **347% increase** of people accessing the site on a mobile browser over 2009 (source: social networking watch)

social networks

it has become increasingly important to have a presence on *social networking* sites like Facebook and MySpace. in addition to these popular *social networks*, there are also many specialised *social networks* that might be the perfect place to create a following for specific products.

social networks not only give the marketer a place to get the word out, they also provide a place to interact with customers and allow customers to interact with each other.

Facebook

1. **Facebook profile:** by creating a profile for yourself or your usiness, you are establishing your identity. this will take you a long way in developing relationships with fellow users and in positioning your business. here are some aspects of a profile page:

- profile picture: always put your best foot forward, which means use the most flattering picture as your profile picture.

- add friends: after creating a profile, don't wait for things to happen. add new friends and the word will spread that you're on Facebook.

- your wall: this is your main platform to interact with Facebook users. post messages on your wall and also comment on members' activities, though, only when relevant.

- photo albums and videos: photos and videos are a great way to showcase the latest collection of your product album.

2. **fan pages:** Facebook pages, known as fan pages, are designed for businesses, brands, companies, products and celebrities. unlike Facebook profiles, pages are visible to everyone on the internet and are generally better for long-term relationships with your fans, readers or customers.

3. **groups:** Facebook groups allow people to come together around a common cause or activity to express their views. one of the best features of groups is the ability to send messages directly to members' Facebook inboxes. groups are generally better for hosting quick active discussions and attracting attention.

4. events: simply put, Facebook events can help you connect with your target audience and invite them for your events, even if they aren't on your friend list or one of your fans. events can be created individually or even from profiles, pages.

5. be unique and keep updating: there's nothing more boring than bland Facebook pages. add lots of personality and fun to your profile. offer something different so that they keep coming back, instead of letting them wait for updates from you.

6. use a big profile picture: who says size doesn't matter? using a big profile picture is one of the best ways to brand your Facebook page. Facebook allows images of up to 200pix wide x 600pix high to be used as profile images pages.

7. tag fans in photos: you can tag your fans in pictures of new collections, or even ask them to tag themselves as a part of a game or contest.

8. exclusive landing page for users: use different pages to target different sets of people. take new users to a page that encourages them to 'Like' you or to a page they would find interesting enough to keep coming back. members/fans can be directed to the wall or a game page that might interest them.

9. reward loyal supporters: encourage loyal supporters to join your page and reward them. tabs or badges like 'member of the month' that can be placed on their profiles for visibility can be awarded to them. a happy customer on Facebook can get you lots of attention.

10. use contests and polls.

the little cook book of social media marketing

11. **actively participate outside your page:** find other Facebook pages related to your industry or topic using Facebook search and start actively commenting on their posts & updates. if you're willing to offer free advice on communities and discussions, it will encourage people to check out your website.

12. **integrate Facebook social plugins to your site:** the 'Like' button on your site enables users to share pages from your site back to their Facebook profile and the 'Recommendation' button gives users of your site personalised suggestions for pages that they like.

13. **marketplace:** with Facebook marketplace, you can buy and sell anything using the listing service.

14. **don't just write for an audience of teenagers:** Facebook isn't filled with youngsters. make sure communicate to your target the right way.

source: http://blog.socialmaximizer.com/14-tips-for-marketing-on-facebook

Facebook statistics

the average user:

- has 130 friends on the site

- sends 8 friend requests per month

- spends an average 15 hours, 33 minutes on Facebook per month

- visits the site 40 times per month

- spends an 23 minutes on each visit

- is connected to 80 community pages, groups and events

- creates 90 pieces of content each month

in general:

- 200 million people access Facebook via a mobile device each day

- more than 30 billion pieces of content are shared each day

- users that access Facebook on mobile devices are twice as active on Facebook compared to non-mobile users

- Facebook generates a staggering 770 billion page views per month

source: facebook.com, pingdom.com – March 2011

the little cook book of social media marketing

MySpace

MySpace is one of the biggest *social media* sites in the world. it has over 250 Million registered users worldwide according to Wikipedia, and growing each day.

1. **MySpace is a social media site:** therefore you need to interact with others. this gives you the chance to know your marketing prospects and take an interest in others and what they have to say.

2. **let people know who you are:** you must open up and let people know who you are, it is not enough to be interested in others. it is OK to talk to people about your business as well, but not all the time.

3. **never over-friend people:** you have the possibility to friend request people with a MySpace account, and this allows you to see their profile and send them messages. keep the friend request under 25 people per day.

4. **keep your marketing about the prospect:** you should always keep your marketing about the prospect, avoid getting into features and details too much. highlight the features that prospects will benefit from.

5. **maintain your MySpace blog:** updating your MySpace blog once per week is not going to work, you must at least make one post per day to your blog. fresh content keeps people interested and coming back for more.

MySpace statistics

- **125 million users** (source: MySpace)

- daily traffic is still over **50 million** - down on 2009 (source: Quantcast)

- male/female ratio is **50:50**

- largest demographic group is **18-34**

- **11.4 million people** access the site via mobile browsers (source: social networking watch)

the little cook book of social media marketing

encyclopaedic networking

one of the few Hawaiian words that have been adop..
internet is wiki. a wiki is a website that allows the creatiu
editing of any number of interlinked web pages via a web brows.
using a simplified markup language or a WYSIWYG editor. wikis
are typically powered by wiki software and are often used
collaboratively by multiple users.

the most popular wiki site is wikipedia – an online, multilingual
social encyclopaedia.

most small businesses and business owners don't qualify for a
wikipedia page, as to qualify the business would have had to have
received some measure of notoriety.

the pros of having a wikipedia article:

1. **great exposure.** wikipedia is a heavily used website, and having
an article about your company means more exposure, more
eyeballs, and so forth.

2. **reputation management.** your Wikipedia article will probably
rank on search engine results page one for your company name,
and that helps with your online reputation management.

3. **increased trust.** there's no underestimating the need to earn
trust, both from customers and search engines. a wikipedia article
can generally help with both.

the cons of a wikipedia article:

1.   **no say in what's said about you**.   even if you qualify for a wikipedia article about your business, wikipedia will frown on you or an employee creating the page, and they'll frown on you even updating or correcting the page.   you don't meet the neutral point of view policy.   you can't make the changes yourself, and this may prove very frustrating.

2.   **it requires constant monitoring**.   if your small business is operating on such a level that you deserve a wikipedia article, there's a chance that you'll have some competition and/or some angry customers or disgruntled employees that would love to make you look bad.   while you can't go in and edit your own wikipedia article, they probably can.

so you have to be extra vigilant in watching for updates and then hope that you can find someone to correct or edit any untruthful information that someone adds.   in some situations, this monitoring can become very time-consuming.

3. **no room for error**. the exposure and notoriety that comes with having a wikipedia article means you have almost no room for error when it comes to future business mistakes.   your ceo makes the news after his picture is taken outside a strip club - that'll show up on your wikipedia page.   or an ex-employee files a discrimination suit against you - that'll show up, too.

source: Matt McGee - http://www.smallbusinesssem.com/should-small-business-have-wikipedia-article

Wikipedia statistics

- **over 3 million** content pages or articles

- **over 12 million** registered users

- the most-wanted Wikipedia articles, as of february 7, 2011:
  1. british films of 2011 (1842)
  2. british films of 2012 (1841)
  3. list of argentine films of 2011 (1712)
  4. bazinaprine (1204)
  5. tetrindole (1203)
  6. sercloremine (1203)
  7. befol (1203)
  8. esuprone (1134)
  9. siddapur, belgaum (1117)
  10. milacemide (1059)

forums

internet forums are the longest established form of online *social media*. They are a discussion area on a website. website members can post discussions and read and respond to posts by other forum members. an internet forum can be focused on nearly any subject and a sense of an online community, or virtual community, tends to develop among forum members. each discussion in a forum is known as a thread, and many different threads can be active simultaneously.

forums are therefore good places to find and engage in a variety of detailed discussions. they are often built into websites as an added feature, but some exist as stand-alone entities. forums can be places for lively, vociferous debate, for seeking advice on a subject, for sharing news, for flirting, or simply for whiling away time with idle chat.

the sites are normally moderated by an administrator, whose role it is to remove unsuitable posts or spam. these moderators will, however, not lead or guide the discussion. this is a major difference between forums and blogs. blogs have a clear owner, whereas a forum's threads are started by its members.

forums have a strong sense of community. some are very enclosed, existing as 'islands' of online social activity with little or no connection to other forms of *social media*. this may be because forums were around long before the term *'social media'* was coined.

the little cook book of social media marketing

an internet forum is also called a message board, discussion group, bulletin board or web forum.   it is also different from a chat room. members in a chat room usually all chat or communicate at the same time, while members in an internet forum post messages to be read by others whenever they happen to log on.   internet forums also tend to be more topic-focused than chat rooms.

business networking

social networking is about one thing: connections. you can join every *social network* on the planet, but unless you can provide some value, some reason for people to want to connect with you, you stand no chance of successfully using *social networking* to make any progress from a business standpoint.

you can use *social networking* sites such as Facebook and MySpace, as outlined earlier. blogging and microblogging are useful business tools, as are bookmarking sites. video and presentation sharing sites also provide a business solution.

the biggest *social networking* site that is centred around business is LinkedIn. it was initially created as a way to connect with your co-workers, business partners, customers, and friends. LinkedIn has become **the** hub for online networking in the more traditional sense – that is business networking – likened to handing out your business card at a cocktail party.

another *business networking* site, with more focus on the social networking is ecademy. set up by Thomas and Penny Power, it combines virtual and physical networking.

other business networking sites include:

- biznik - a community of entrepreneurs and small businesses dedicated to helping each other succeed.

- cmypitch - a business website for UK entrepreneurs to get quotes, advice and more.

- Cofoundr - a community for entrepreneurs, programmers, designers, investors, and other individuals involved with starting new ventures.

- E.Factor - an online community and virtual marketplace designed for entrepreneurs, by entrepreneurs.

- Entrepreneur Connect – a community by entrepreneur.com where professionals can network, communicate, and collaborate with others.

- Fast Pitch – a business network where professionals can market their business and make connections.

- PartnerUp – a community connecting small business owners and entrepreneurs.

- XING – a european business network with more than 7 million members.

- Ziggs – a professional connection portal founded on the principles of professionalism and respect.

LinkedIn

LinkedIn is a very different environment than the other social networking sites. that means that you will need to take advantage of it in a different manner.

- firstly, create your own personal profile on LinkedIn.

- connect with all of your business acquaintances that you can find.   connect with old classmates, professors, and co-workers and build a network.

- LinkedIn allows you to join 50 groups, so join 50 groups. these will preferably be groups that have to do with your industry.

- answer questions. LinkedIn has a questions and answers section where users can ask people questions about a given topic.

- if you are open to connecting with just about anyone one LinkedIn (a great way to build new connections). considering adding the term LION after your name (this stands for LinkedIn Open Networker), which means you are willing to connect with anyone that asks to connect with you.

LinkedIn statistics

- site traffic is up in the recession

- has over **60 million** members (feb 2010 – source: TechCrunch)

- new members are joining at a rate of approx. **one new member per second**

- doubled monthly unique visitors in the year, to **7.7 million** (scource: ComScore)

- took 477 days to reach its first million members. The 60th million took only **12 days** (oct 2009)

social bookmarking

social bookmarking is the practice of saving bookmarks to a public website and "tagging" them with keywords. bookmarking, on the other hand, is the practice of saving the address of a website you wish to visit in the future on your computer.

visitors to social bookmarking sites can search for resources by keyword, person, or popularity and see the public bookmarks, tags, and classification schemes that registered users have created and saved.

activities like social bookmarking give users the opportunity to express differing perspectives on information and resources through informal organisational structures. this allows like-minded individuals to find each other and create new communities of users.

the most popular social bookmarking sites are:

- Twitter
- Digg
- Reddit
- StumbleUpon
- Delicious
- TweetMeMe
- Mixx
- FARK
- Slashdot
- FriendFeed
- ClipMarks
- NewsVine
- Diligo
- Hacker News
- BlinkList

video networking

video-sharing sites allow you to upload and share your personal videos with the rest of the web community.

some of the most effective *social media marketing* strategies centre around YouTube and viral marketing videos.

while this can often be more time-consuming and expensive, YouTube can easily become the centrepiece of a larger *social media* campaign.

video networking provides marketers with the opportunity to demonstrate with customers.   how-to videos, spoof adverts and niche communications are common on this medium.

YouTube statistics

- **2nd largest search engine**, after google. it surpassed Yahoo! in august 2008

- US internet users watched **32.4 billion videos** in January 2010

- YouTube accounted for nearly **99%** of all those videos (source: ComScore)

the little cook book of social media marketing

social media marketing

social media marketing is a mechanism to interact with a set of online *social media* conversations from a marketing perspective, based on converged media (since conversations span technologies and media).

interaction is key – you must create an atmosphere in which dialogue is encouraged and open. as marketers always want to control the message, you must enable the right messages to develop – this requires monitoring and control, but also openness randomness and support.

social media marketing is measurable via a set of *social media* metrics.   based on the data driven dials of this interface, the marketer monitors these many way conversations.

marketers benchmark the insights gained from these conversations against a set of transactional data (sales, surveys, etc) to monitor and tweak a series of specific campaigns.

instead of having one large 'broadcast' campaign - we have many small narrowcast, interactive and ongoing campaigns.   the campaigns and conversations are based on a feedback loop, hence they are iterative and form an ongoing learning experience.

social media marketing mix

actors: people or members

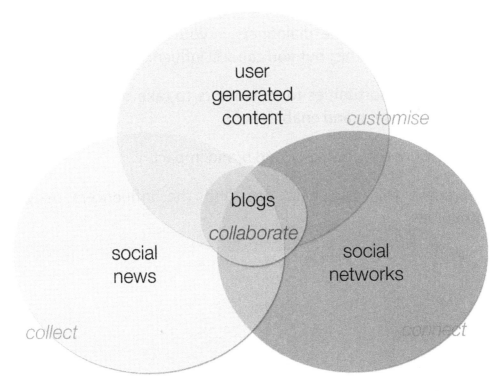

source: fuordigital – www.slideshare.com

networks - connect people, allowing an interaction with technology and other people, albeit virtually.

news – collects information to consume it or to reuse it in its entirety or in pieces.

user generated content – people customise the information to suit their purpose – taking from the news collection and distributing it within their networks.

people are talking about your brand now!

1. start by using tools to **measure** the noise

2. **immerse** yourself in the conversation/s

3. **participate** in the dialogue/s.   you will have to relinquish control to do this, but you can still influence

4. create opportunities for customers to take **ownership** of the brand. inspire and enable them

5. **measure** the new noise and brand impact

this process will also help you find the influencers in your communities.

the little cook book of social media marketing

measurement tools

many social media analytics tools are free to use. these include:

- Blogpulse
  a blog search engine that also allows analyses and reports to be created on the daily activities in the blogosphere.

- Twist.com
  for searching Twitter.

- Trendrr
  a campaign, term or brand is entered and tracked.

- Technorati
  a self-service advertising network of blogs.

other, paid services also provide analytics tools:

- ScoutLabs
  tracks what customers love and hate about brands, and engage with influential customers for new product development and marketing ideas.

- Nielson BuzzMetrics
  helps companies measure, understand and leverage the increasing amount of consumer activity, influence and content - the "buzz" - that was migrating to the internet and new forms of media.

- Collective Intellect
  produces real time market intelligence to monitor and analyse conversations and mentions on social media sites

the little cook book of social media marketing

conclusion

"
what used to be cigarette breaks could turn into 'social media breaks' as long as there is a clear signal and IT isn't looking.
"

David Armano

social media marketing is all about engagement – your audience become friends, and your friends become customers. the media allows companies to build trust and reputation in the marketplace, and create a buzz about your brand and products.

people buy from their friends...

so be a friend

about the author

Thom Poole is a professional chartered marketer who has spent his career in developing customer-centric products and services.

during the course of writing his dissertation for his *marketing* masters, Thom identified trust as being a key factor in business success, forming the basis of his first book '*Play It By Trust*'.

with a long relationship with digital *marketing*, Thom has worked for some of the most innovative global companies, as an employee and consultant.

a professor of *marketing* at Grenoble, Thom has also created the first MSc in digital *marketing*, being delivered by a London business school.

this book was written to provide a quick guide to helping individuals and businesses understand the elements, impact and benefits of *marketing*.

understanding and quantifying *marketing* is an ongoing task, and this book is only one step on the journey.

for more information, please visit Thom's websites:

www.jack-marketing.com

www.about-marketing.co.uk

other titles in the howto marketing series:

Principles of Marketing	Product Marketing
Price Marketing	Promotional Marketing
e-Promotional Marketing	Web Marketing
NPD Marketing	International Marketing
Marketing Planning	Marketing Audits
Customer Relationship Marketing	Mobile Marketing
Web Design for the Terrified	Direct Marketing
Search Engine Marketing	The Little Cook Book of Trust
The Little Cook Book of Marketing	

Lightning Source UK Ltd.
Milton Keynes UK
UKOW05f1041190416

272540UK00010B/368/P